WILDLIFE IN BLOOM SERIES

Little Squirrel

BY AUTHOR & CONSERVATIONIST

LINDA BLACKMOOR

ISBN: 978-1-966417-25-5 (PRINT)

PUBLISHED BY QUILL PRESS. LINDA BLACKMOOR'S TITLES MAY BE PURCHASED IN BULK FOR EDUCATIONAL, BUSINESS, FUNDRAISING, OR SALES PROMOTIONAL USE. FOR INFORMATION, PLEASE EMAIL HELLO@LINDABLACKMOOR.COM

FIRST PRINT EDITION: 2025

LINDA BLACKMOOR
WWW.LINDABLACKMOOR.COM

SPECIES

Squirrels are rodents in the Sciuridae family, which includes tree squirrels, ground squirrels, and flying squirrels. There are over 200 species of squirrels found worldwide, except in Antarctica and Australia. Their scientific name, Sciurus, comes from Greek words meaning "shadow tail," referring to their bushy tails. Squirrels have adapted to ecosystems, from tropical rainforests to arctic tundra.

LOOKS

Most squirrels have furred tails nearly as long as their bodies, helping them balance while climbing. Their front paws each have four fingers, while their hind paws have five, providing a powerful grip on branches. Fur colors range from red, gray, and brown to pure black or white, depending on species and environment. They have large eyes, aiding in depth perception when leaping between branches.

HABITAT

Tree squirrels thrive in woodlands, parks, and suburban areas with plenty of trees for nesting. Ground squirrels live in burrows across prairies, deserts, and mountainous regions, often in large colonies. Flying squirrels inhabit forests, gliding between trees on membranes of skin between their front and back legs. Their habitat choice depends on food availability, shelter, and safety.

TYPES

Popular types of squirrels include the Eastern Gray Squirrel in North America, Red Squirrel in Europe, and Malabar Giant Squirrel in India. Flying squirrels like the Southern Flying Squirrel glide up to 300 feet between trees. Ground squirrels such as prairie dogs and chipmunks are closely related, though they look and behave differently. Each type has unique features and behaviors suited to its region.

DIET

Squirrels are primarily omnivores, though most eat seeds, nuts, and fruits as the bulk of their diet. They also consume insects, small birds' eggs, and fungi when available, providing extra protein. Some species store nuts for winter, burying them in hidden caches to dig up later. This variety in diet helps squirrels adapt to changing seasons and habitats.

SQUIRREL FACTS #6

CHEWING

A squirrel's front teeth (incisors) grow continuously, at a rate of about 6 inches (15 cm) per year if left unchecked. Chewing on nuts, bark, and other tough materials grinds them down naturally, preventing overgrowth. Their strong bite helps them crack open hard shells like acorns and hickory nuts. Good dental health is vital for them to access diverse food sources.

FORAGE

Squirrels are expert foragers, constantly searching for seeds, nuts, and other treats. They bury or hide surplus food in tree cavities and underground caches, returning later for a meal. Some forget about these hidden stashes, allowing buried seeds to sprout into new plants. By spreading seeds far and wide, squirrels aid forest regeneration and plant diversity.

VOCALS

Squirrels chatter, squeak, and use tail flicks to warn others of predators and express excitement or aggression. They also release scent markers to claim territory and communicate readiness to mate. Flying squirrels use ultrasonic calls (too high for humans to hear) to keep track of one another at night. This mix of cues helps maintain social bonds and safety.

NESTS

Tree-dwelling squirrels build dreys, round nests made of twigs, leaves, and moss, often placed in tree forks. Some use natural hollows in trunks for added protection from weather and predators. Ground squirrels dig burrows with tunnels and chambers for sleeping, storing food, and rearing young. Cozy nesting spots keep them warm in cold climates and serve as safe nurseries for offspring.

WINTER

Although squirrels don't hibernate fully, some enter a state of torpor, reducing activity to conserve energy in cold weather. Tree squirrels rely on food caches to survive when fresh nuts and seeds become scarce. Ground squirrels may sleep for extended periods, occasionally waking to eat stored food. Preparation in fall is key, ensuring they have enough supplies to survive winter.

SQUIRREL FACTS #11

PREDATOR

Common squirrel predators include hawks, owls, snakes, foxes, and domestic cats. Squirrels rely on their agility, keen eyesight, and quick reflexes to avoid capture. Tree squirrels scurry up trunks in a spiral motion, staying on the opposite side of the predator. Flying squirrels can leap away and glide to safety, while ground squirrels retreat into burrows.

SOCIAL

While some squirrels live solitary lives, others, like ground squirrels, gather in colonies to share warning calls. Flying squirrels occasionally roost together in groups to stay warm, especially during colder months. In tree-dwelling species, dominant males may defend territories where females nest. Social interactions and group living vary widely, reflecting each species' survival strategy.

LIFESPAN

In the wild, squirrels typically live 3 to 6 years, facing threats from predators, traffic, and habitat loss. In protected environments or captivity, they can reach 10 years or more with steady food and fewer dangers. Eastern Gray Squirrels are known for their adaptability, often outliving other species in suburban settings. Each year of survival helps squirrels contribute to seed dispersal and forest health.